THE JOY OF MINIMALISM

A Beginner's Guide to Happiness with Less

ZOEY ARIELLE POULSEN

For permission requests, please contact the publisher at:
Mango Publishing Group
2850 Douglas Road, 3rd Floor
Coral Gables, FL 33134 USA
info@mango.bz

For special orders, quantity sales, course adoptions and corporate sales, please email the publisher at sales@mango.bz. For trade and wholesale sales, please contact Ingram Publisher Services at customer.service@ingramcontent.com or +1.800.509.4887.

The Joy of Minimalism: A Beginner's Guide to the Simple Life and the Pursuit of Happiness

Library of Congress Cataloging
ISBN: (print) 978-1-63353-689-0, (ebook) 978-1-63353-687-6
Library of Congress Control Number: 2017959857
BISAC category code: CRA005000 CRAFTS & HOBBIES / Decorating
SEL016000 SELF-HELP / Personal Growth / Happiness

Printed in the United States of America

"Clutter is not just physical stuff. It's old ideas, toxic relationships and bad habits. Clutter is anything that does not support your better self."

— **Eleanor Brownn**, Author of *Mile 9*

TABLE OF CONTENTS

I

INTRODUCTION

AN HONEST INTRODUCTION

I want to start off this book by saying thank you. Thank you for picking it up and giving it an honest chance. Perhaps you found me on YouTube and have been following me for a while, or this book somehow caught your eye at a bookstore, and for that I thank you. Everything happens for a reason, and I truly believe that if you are open to it, this book will change your life in a positive way (or hopefully in many ways)!

At this time, the videos I post on YouTube about minimalism are the most popular on my channel. As a video gains momentum on YouTube, it is bound to be seen by an audience that is not necessarily your target, or in other words, not your "tribe." My ideal audience/tribe is made up of positive self-improvement junkies, because hey, that's me. YouTube trolls (or "haters") can throw a lot of shade, but I hope that sharing my minimalism journey will help you do at least one of the following: diminish anxiety, make money, save money, declutter your home, declutter your mind, and most importantly, allow you to have more of life's most precious resource: time—time to spend with family and friends, or to finally pursue the business endeavor you have always had on the back burner in your mind.

I struggled for weeks and even months with trying to put together how I wanted to communicate my minimalism tips and journey in book form because of the backlash I have received on YouTube. Unfortunately, there will always be someone in the world who will disagree with you, but fortunately, the journey of minimalism and of life is all your own. As long as you are happy and fully content with the choices you are making on a daily basis, you are living an authentic life. I hope this book will expand your views and allow you to adjust or change your lens on how you view material items and your precious time and how you feel about them. By learning to let go and limit what you obtain, you will be able to gain more than ever imagined. I refer to this positive life gain as *fulfillment*.

To me, minimalism and this book are about the concept of simplification in different areas of your life, such as your wardrobe or your home—making room for what matters most to *you* specifically. Minimizing my life has allowed happiness to come more easily on a daily basis, and I know that if you open your mind while closing the lid on your spending habits, it will do the same for you.

Let's get started!

WHAT IS MINIMALISM?

A journey.

Minimalism is not living out of a suitcase, only owning a certain number of items, living in a tiny house, or only owning white furniture. Minimalism can certainly be these things, but is not limited to them. The journey of minimalism is about becoming conscious of the world around you, simplifying your life, and actively choosing to incorporate only the things in your life which bring you joy. Thus, this journey is unique to everyone.

We are all different human beings and will always be different human beings. You may LOVE cilantro so much that you would plant a lawn of it in your front yard just so you could smell it every day, whereas your best friend may despise cilantro so much that if a stem found its way into her taco, the whole restaurant would know about it.

You may love golden retrievers, yet your aunt may refuse to even pet dogs, though she owns twenty cats.

Your younger brother may love video games, but you may strongly feel your eyes would burn out attempting to play with him for even fifteen minutes.

We are all different.

And that is okay.

Our differences and uniqueness make the world go 'round. How boring would life be if we all enjoyed the same things, partook in the same activities, and ate the same food?

For your hypothetical friend's sake, let's hope that this kind of world would say "no" to cilantro.

Minimalism is about reclaiming your time in life to do more of the things which add irreplaceable value to you personally, such as spending more time with your family or focusing more on your health. Once you discover the true value of time and the joy it can bring you, you will realize life is better lived enjoying every day through moments, rather than trying to find enjoyment through things.

BECOMING A MINIMALIST: MY JOURNEY

Perhaps I was born a minimalist—I mean, I *did* arrive on this earth as a naked screaming bundle of joy. I didn't feel the automatic need to go out and clothe myself in designer goods, purchase something to feel endorphins, or own the latest iPhone to prove I was successful in life—I simply wanted to be held. I think that is the case for each and every one of us.

9

Society, our upbringing, and the media are what sway us to accumulate "stuff" to become happier. The average person is exposed to hundreds of advertisements every single day. Having had a career in marketing, I can say hands down that the goal of marketing is to persuade you to purchase something, regardless of whether it is ethical or not. Thus, the hundreds of advertisements we are exposed to per day are often successful in communicating that we will be happier by purchasing more. Somehow, we expect that by filling our makeup bags, closets, and homes with things, happiness will burst through the door like the Kool-Aid jug character, screaming "OH YEAAAH!" This, however, is not reality.

Brands succeed in selling to us by taking the time to research what our society is interested in and what sparks people's excitement or attention. In turn, we as consumers spend hours and hours researching products and reading product reviews, and we have no problem spending a full day walking around the mall. We swipe our credit cards and check our bank account balances, yet how many of us take the time to explore whether we are actually balanced and happy?

Here's a brief introduction to how I got sucked into the bubble of materialism, floated around in it for the majority of my life, and then popped it—only to realize how little it actually took to become fulfilled in life.

While I was growing up, I was pushed by my parents to spend the majority of my time outdoors: bike riding, playing road hockey, or building forts with my brothers. My fondest memories are of camping on Vancouver Island and running around the backyard with my cousins; we truly didn't need much more than our imaginations to have a good time. I was always taught to enjoy simplicity, respect the outdoors, and work for what I wanted. I was never one of those children who asked for a new possession and expected it to be given without any effort. Thank you, Dad.

In elementary school, I began to become aware of the "outside world", and with that came influencers: friends, the media, The Spice Girls, etc. Those were exciting times for sure —discovering new worlds that were so very different from my own. I often daydreamed about what it would be like to wear sparkling outfits and platform shoes. I also felt a little envy growing up with the belief that I might never be able to obtain some of the possessions I dreamt about, because my parents would never buy them for me and/or I would not be able to afford them myself.

However, things changed when I landed my first "real job" working as a courtesy clerk (yes, a bagging-and-buggy girl) at a local grocery store. Having my own paycheck meant the money I made was mine to spend.

I would wait patiently for my biweekly paychecks, already planning out where every dollar and cent was going to go the moment it was deposited. I'd spend my money on clothes, DVDs, food—basically, anything I wanted—and I felt a thrill with every purchase because I was in control of it; I had newfound freedom.

I spent my free time on day trips to the mall with my friends. I always enjoyed seeing how many things I could purchase with my latest paycheck. If I saw shirts on sale at a good price, such as two shirts for ten dollars, you bet I had to jump on that deal. The phrase "the more you buy, the more you save" was a little too familiar to me.

Of course, once high school came, materialism hit a new level when name-brand clothing became a "must" to fit in and when I finally got my driver's license. The pressure was on as a teenager—somehow it felt necessary to prove my wealth as a person by displaying it any way that I could.

Next came the university, where I had to make new friends —what better way to make new friends than having nice, new clothing? Along with copious amounts of clothing came furnishing a flat, buying a new car, and a bunch of other junk I can't even remember now.

When I was twenty years old, in the summer before my final year at University, I went backpacking through Europe by myself. The experience was nothing less than transformative; and it completely blows my mind now, as I can't imagine how I managed the adventure alone with paper maps and without a cellphone (first world problems, I know).

During this adventure of mine, I was able to find myself to an extent I never had before. Apparently, the real Zoey was hidden somewhere underneath an excess of clothes and possessions, and all she needed to be discovered was a backpack and a map of Europe. During this time abroad, I pulled back the layers of materialism in my life and was able to explore pure authenticity.

Had I been aloof my whole life?

Stepping foot onto the Copenhagen-bound plane in Vancouver meant that the journey ahead of me was my time to explore the world and myself on my own. While I was away from my life in Canada, I realized what made me feel alive and fulfilled. To my surprise, it wasn't my new car, it wasn't my boyfriend, it wasn't shopping; it was *adventure*.

Throughout my travels, I didn't feel a need to shop my way through Europe—I simply wanted to spend the money I had on special and memorable experiences. (*Who was this girl?*) Once I started to taste the freedom of real-life adventure, I yearned for cultural moments and significant conversations. I was observing, discovering, and transforming. Spending time with my family in Denmark also introduced me to the Scandinavian aesthetic: clean, airy, and simple—I noticed the benefits to my mind immediately. Stepping into a minimalist home instantly felt stress-free, breathable, and open. These spaces were like nothing I had ever seen before in North America. I remember scribbling notes into the back of my journal like, "*What I want my future house to look like: white, with nothing but a little bit of simple luxury inside.*" It's true what everyone says about Hygge in Denmark, it is the coziest feeling.

While I was away, I forgot about the things that I owned that weren't in the contents of my nylon backpack; when I returned to Canada, I felt overwhelmed by my belongings. I had countless clothes that I had forgotten I had, some still with tags, jewelry I kept for what I thought were sentimental reasons, and more than enough furniture for my means. Truthfully, I had no real relationship with any of my possessions—I had forgotten about them all. I realized that, over the span of my life, I had accumulated too many belongings—more than I could manage, clean, or take care of.

I felt like a hoarder, even though I was not even close to some of the people I had seen on the reality TV shows about hoarding. I felt overwhelmed because I realized I had consumed so many things that weren't necessarily providing benefit to me, or even enjoyment. While on my journey, I had seen people who had so much less than I did, yet who were extremely content with their lives. These countless observations gave rise to the large and unignorable question of "*why?*"

Despite this, when I had settled back in at home and felt spontaneous enough to get rid of all my belongings, I somehow suppressed my intuition and fell back into my old patterns. My cycle included going into hibernation mode while burying myself in studies and work, then transitioning away and racing like a mad woman to buy anything I could get my hands on that would give me a pick-me-up.

Shopping was like my espresso after a rough night's sleep, only I felt like I was sleeping my way through life and like I needed a lot more than an espresso to cure it. Shopping for clothing, makeup, or other products was addictive to me like a drug, especially during stressful times at university (when as a student I really did not have the funds for such a lifestyle). The new purchases lost their sparkle after a few rounds, and then, like a junkie, I'd find myself at the mall again or filling my online shopping cart. I was, and I felt, *out of control*.

Although my habits were a little ridiculous, there was one major aspect of my Euro trip mental shift which did stick with me through the remainder of my studies, and that was quality over quantity. I realized in the past I had been drawn to sale items that I didn't necessarily love, but would purchase because I felt a deal was too good to pass up, even if the clothing tended to fall apart after only a couple of washes. Those were the items which hung in my closet, tags still on. I made the decision moving forward that from then on in my life, I would only acquire good quality pieces.

The next chapter of my life was moving to the big city of Toronto. The new city, the new way of life, and the corporate climbing around me made me feel I needed to obtain a new level of business clothes. Swipe here, swipe there—the plastic was getting hot as I went for quality over quantity, yet I still felt I needed to obtain a lot of it: *What would people think if I wore the same blazer twice in one week?*

The truth was and is: *it does not matter*.

Whether or not a new style was expensive, somehow I felt I needed to obtain it for my collection to feel good and successful, when really, I was just contributing to financial stress in my life. The more I thought consciously about my shopping habits, the more I found going to the mall tiresome. The further I got into the marketing world, the clearer the illusions became, and I began to feel overwhelmed by all the marketing going on around me. I also realized the only time I seemed to want to go to the mall was when I had had a mediocre day at work, because *a new lipstick or new shirt was sure to fix my day and my unfulfilling corporate position, wasn't it?* Unfortunately, mediocre days at work occurred all too often.

From the discomfort of my desk, I yearned for adventure every day. I wanted to hop on a plane back to Europe and indulge in the beauty of culture: art, food, language, etc. Although these thoughts were on my mind daily, I didn't quite make the connection that that was how I would personally achieve lasting, fulfilling happiness.

Europe felt more and more out of my reach as I continued to suffocate myself in my limiting beliefs: *"You can't move there, it's impossible";* or *"You have built too much of a life here to leave it";* or *"Who are you to quit your job?"*

I yearned to rediscover my lust for life, shed my limiting beliefs about my potential for happiness, and buy that plane ticket.

It was in my darkest voids that I realized it was my baggage that was literally weighing me down, baggage in the sense of having a fully furnished apartment, student loans, and a whole lot of things—or for lack of a better word, "junk."

Minimalism was then and still is an inward journey, a journey that was necessary for me to discover myself and what sparks joy within my soul. The journey has inspired and still inspires me to take my life to the next level every day. It gave me the ability to rekindle my lust for life and allowed me to follow my adventurous dreams.

"Rock bottom was the solid foundation on which I rebuilt my life."

— J.K. Rowling

By no means does one have to hit rock bottom to bring themselves to discover minimalism and the joy the journey brings, but one does have to do the internal work. This "work" refers to the daily exercises we all know we should do, but can't seem to fit it into our schedules: journaling, meditation, fitness, etc. If journaling takes only five minutes per day or meditation takes ten, why do we find this so difficult?

If you want a radical change in your life, you need to do the work required to take that internal journey.

Perhaps it is so easy for us to swipe our credit cards for a possession because someone else created it, and we did not have to put any of our own time into the idea or manufacturing process. We so willingly and easily incorporate material possessions into our existence, but find it so difficult to identify within our own souls what sparks joy within. When you think about this from an outside perspective, it doesn't make any sense, because investing in the creation of the future we most desire deserves our undivided attention. Who doesn't desire a life without financial stressors, clutter, or excess baggage? The inward journey is needed in order to recognize this and make it happen.

When I finally recognized my low point for what it was, I was able to identify what I had been trying to mask with possessions and clutter all along: I wanted to be in *Rome, Italy*.

Once I knew what my goal was, I held the idea so clearly in my mind that if I were to rid myself of all the clutter in my life and downsize my possessions, possibly to the size of a suitcase, I would be able to fly away—all the way to Rome.

And that is exactly what I did.

Walking through the streets of Rome paints a smile on my face that no new dress ever gave me, and tasting a meal I put together with fresh market produce makes me feel more vibrant than any new facial products ever could. I no longer feel as if I need to keep up with the media or those around me through the attainment of material possessions, for I know I have achieved bliss all on my own. I am content with living a life with less, and more importantly, I am content with myself.

When one does not rely on the external world and all of its possessions to bring happiness, life becomes more vivid and meaningful, and in turn gratitude fills the soul.

WHAT MAKES YOU HAPPY IN LIFE?

Where are those moments that bring out the best in you hiding? Do they come out when you have one-on-one time with your children? When you're on a runner's high in the wilderness?

Surfing the perfect wave? Working on a creative business endeavor? Helping animals?

You owe it to yourself to live your best life.

What is a life lived with what-ifs?

It is unfulfilled, empty of all the things you would have preferred to spend your time on.

The minimalism process is about taking the time to discover your bliss and decluttering everything around you enough to feel happiness through the abundance of time and meaningful experiences rather than of material possessions.

Perhaps travel or moving to your dream city isn't what will bring you personal bliss, but ask yourself where your mind would go if you could open up the top of your head and pull out all the stressors in your life. Would you be tending to your own farm? Working with children? Baking your heart out?

Take the next few pages to write about what it would be like to follow your bliss and achieve joy. Don't forget to make it as visual as possible.

An example could be: *If I had all the time and resources in the world, I would spend my days baking in my dream kitchen. The sunlight would pour through the window and grant me the perfect glow for reading through my recipe notes. My gaze would meander across a green field to the forest beyond as the occasional deer wandered past....*

_____

_____

_____

_____

_____

_____

_____

_____

_____

_____

_____

_____

_____

_____

_____

_____

_____

_____

_____

_____

_____

_____

_____

_____

_____

_____

If I had discovered the journey of minimalism sooner, I could have taken control of my life and drawn closer to my dreams a lot sooner. I want this book to do exactly that for you. I want it to influence you to become more conscious, to be inspired to rid yourself of the excess baggage you carry materially, mentally, and emotionally, and to discover what it is that makes you feel fulfilled and happy. Once you understand what that spark is made of and actively choose to simplify your life, it is only a matter of time before what fulfills you becomes your new reality.

I believe in you—now it's time for *you* to believe in you.

II

HOW-TO

BECOMING A MINIMALIST

So I've inspired you to keep reading—and you want to become a minimalist! Great! Start calling yourself one.

As mentioned previously, your definition of minimalism is unique to you and your inward and personal journey. The more you grasp this concept and decide to take serious action and define yourself as a minimalist, the easier the decluttering process will become, and before you know it, the benefits will flood into your life.

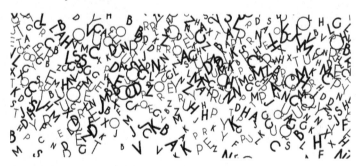

BECOMING CONSCIOUS

Have you ever noticed how once you get to know a person, they can become ten times hotter or ten times more unattractive, depending on their personality and how they make you feel? Soon that will be how you view products and advertisements.

Marketing has a dark side, in the sense that it encourages us to fill our internal voids with temporary fixes. However, it is up to us not to fall into the daily traps, like being swayed to purchase a pretty new dress we saw on Instagram just because we have an engagement party coming up and no partner in our lives to attend it with.

It is time to awaken from the bubble of materialism and realize you do not need to obtain material items to boost your confidence, your lust for life, or your happiness. The items you choose to bring into your life should only be those with which you have truly fallen in love. Possessions you choose to incorporate into your life should align with your authentic self and spark joy inside of you.

In the past, I used to be a serious victim of "fast fashion." I would get excited about seeing a clothing rack displaying signs like, "SALE" or "2 for $10!" I would race to these racks and try to like something enough to buy it, especially if the previous price was a lot more than the current numbers on the sale tag. Brand names over comfort, fit, and realistic personal style, right? *Nope.*

The more I acquired, the better deal I thought I was getting. What I failed to realize was that in reality, I was creating a collection of clothing that I didn't love or rarely wore, or which fell apart after a wash or two.

Let me ask you a little question: Would you invite a "discount" significant other into your life? For example, a lover who has a cool name, but who you don't like spending time with, talking to, or who is never there for you?

I sure hope you answered "no".

Use this question the next time you see a sale rack. Do not to invite anything into your life which is not 150% you or what you deserve. You deserve to only bring things into your life that make you smile ear to ear and spark joy within your soul. When it comes to clothes or products, they need to align with you and make you feel comfortable, stylish, confident, and authentic.

Start adjusting your lens, look a little deeper into the world of consumerism, and begin to uncover the somewhat hidden reality of it all. When a commercial says you will be classier with a new watch, don't let it phase you. You and I both know a person is classy if they have good manners and carry themselves well, not just because they have the latest arm candy. You are perfect just the way you are; be authentic to yourself, and screw anyone who tries to tell you otherwise. Next time you see a commercial claiming you need to make sure you have the softest skin by obtaining X, Y, and Z products—reevaluate. Happiness is a state of being, not having.

Once you begin to look around and feel untouched by billboards or by magazine and Instagram ads, life becomes simpler, and as an added benefit, your wallet becomes a whole lot fatter.

Take the time now to write down why you feel the urge to purchase new or more specifically brand name possessions:

Examples could be:

To impress the opposite sex.
To make a good impression on my coworkers.
To show my neighbors I am successful.

(FYI: This exercise is intended to leave you feeling a little bit silly after you read what you have written down.)

_____

_____

_____

_____

_____

_____

_____

_____

_____

_____

_____

_____

_____

_____

_____

_____

Now that we have examined the urges that cause impulse buying, it is time to defeat them. Consumerism is meant to target our insecurities. Marketers want to sell, sell, sell, and too often the way they achieve this is to make us feel like we are less without their products.

I am here to affirm to you that you do not need them, everything you need, you have within yourself. Celebrate your uniqueness as a human being and take the time now to reflect on your self. Reflect on the insecurities or flaws you believe you have, and counter them with a powerful statements about yourself with at least three positive points in the following pages. Facing our insecurities head on in the form of journalling will assist in defeating them once and for all! By being able to defeat our insecurities and feel more confidence within ourselves, we will defeat our needs to purchase more to cover up the "flaws" we keep convincing ourselves of.

An example could be:

Insecurity: *I have always felt self-concious of the mole on my face. Often times when I see cosmetic surgeries being advertised I consider one day getting it removed.*

Positive counter statements: *I love the mole on my face, in fact, from now on I am going to refer to it as my "beauty mark!" My beauty mark is unique to me, and I have never met another with the same mark. My grandmother, who is one of my greatest inspirations, has continually reminded me that "back in the day," many famous actresses painted little moles on their faces to achieve the unique beauty-mark-look I have been so lucky to have been born with.*

_____

_____

_____

_____

_____

_____

_____

_____

_____

_____

_____

_____

_____

_____

_____

_____

_____

_____

_____

_____

_____

_____

_____

_____

_____

In the previous pages you might have cried and/or you may have laughed. Often by taking the time to write out and acknowledge the thoughts in our head we realize they can be quite silly! Don't let those pesky marketers prey on your silliness. While we're at it, give yourself a pat on the back; You just took the time to actively learn about yourself and boost your own self-confidence.

By continuing to practice exercises such as this one you will begin to understand we do not need to become dependent on material possessions to grant us happiness, fulfilment or self-confidence. Become conscious and stay conscious!

WHY BEGIN?

Willpower comes from within.

By this point in your life, you can identify the times when you stuck with something because you truly loved it, and can also recall times when you gave something up or quit because it wasn't right for you.

The beautiful thing about minimalism is that it's essence is the concept of simplification, which, as mentioned previously, means something different for every person. If you have made it this far into this book, there is at least one specific reason why you wish to pursue a journey in minimalism, and that is going to be your continual source of motivation. Whether your reasons have to do with family, friends, health, fitness, business, etc.— whatever your top reason is, hold it in your mind.

As you keep simplifying your life and drawing closer to this desired goal, you will begin to become aware of different aspects of the journey which are beneficial to you. For example, when I first began my journey, I was looking to simplify my possessions down to the size of a suitcase because my ultimate goal was to move to Rome, Italy. During the downsizing process I became more creative, more organized, tidier, more productive, more financially stable, etc. I also began to pay closer attention to the people I was surrounding myself with and realized I had some decluttering to do in the friends' department as well, but more on that later. These were only a few of the benefits that ultimately led me to my goal.

Begin now for unlimited benefits in your own life.

III

THE FIRST STEP

GET INSPIRED

What initially inspired you to learn more about minimalism? Were you scrolling through Pinterest one day or clicking through to a new world on YouTube? Did you stumble across a documentary on Netflix or visit a Scandinavian furniture store? Whatever sparked your interest in the concepts at first, take a mental note, and keep reminding yourself about what fueled your initial inspiration.

If you are the type of person who may need more than a mental note to stay inspired, take the time to create a specific board on Pinterest, make your own vision board for your success, or change your desktop wallpaper to a chic, minimal living room. Whatever it takes to stay inspired, stay on top of it!

STOP EXPANSION

In addition to the first steps of becoming more conscious and getting inspired, I advise that your next actionable step be stopping expansion in your life. Stopping expansion refers to putting the brakes on the flow of possessions into your life. This could mean not shopping for clothes for the next month, not allowing yourself to purchase any accessories, or simply refraining from buying anything else you do not *need*.

It is best to stop the flow of belongings into your life until you have decluttered your space enough to become aware of the benefits. The more you begin to feel refreshed, light, and free, the more you will be turned off from bringing anything new or foreign into your home.

This journey will take time and a little getting used to. It will require you to pay closer attention to your mind and to what captivates its attention.

Begin to recognize feelings of temptation when they present themselves. What actions, images, and people make you feel like you need to acquire more in life? Perhaps it is just an invitation to an event; for example, in the past, when I was invited to a birthday, wedding, or special event, I instantly felt the need to go out and purchase a new dress or lipstick— anything to help me feel different or fancy.

The truth was, I had many items in my closet suitable for a wedding, such as a little black dress. However, because of my habitual shopping as well as societal norms and pressures, I felt it would be inappropriate to wear a dress I had previously worn to a birthday when attending a wedding, or vice versa.

I can promise you it is now a relief to know I can go home and find exactly what I need the instant I receive an invitation to an event. It is also a major relief to no longer feel affected by advertisements for the latest trends in the streets or in stores. I enjoy my capsule wardrobe enough to know that simple pieces, such as a little black dress which can be dressed up or down, are keystones. There is no need for wardrobe expansion when you know, love, and feel comfortable with what you already have.

TAKE NOTE OF YOUR ROUTINE

With your new minimalist lens on, begin to take time to observe your daily routines. How are you spending your mornings, afternoons, and evenings? Does your routine actually entail using the material items surrounding you?

For example, if you always eat oatmeal for breakfast, yet own a toaster that never gets used, free up that space on your counter top by donating the toaster to someone who actually eats toast for breakfast. Toast can not only be made in a toaster, but also in a toaster oven or even in the oven. Begin to challenge yourself to decipher which of your household appliances you can do without.

challenge yourself

These simple actions allow you to live more consciously each day. You will begin to notice the things surrounding you which add value to your life and those which add little to no value. The items which add no value are actually taking away from you in the form of space and time. It is time for you to reclaim your most precious resource.

BEGIN REDUCING THE CLUTTER

Here comes the fun part! Really—be excited.

Take a mental note of cluttered spaces around you. A great place to start is by doing "surface checks." Surface checks include doing a scan of all table tops, counters, dresser tops, etc. All surfaces that are visible in the home should be clear of clutter. Clutter brings with it anxiety and overwhelm, so begin your journey by decreasing the visible clutter around you first. Once you have worked through one room, take part in a small exercise to spark motivation and bask in the pride of a job well done: step out of the room and walk back in with fresh eyes. Note of all the visible changes you have just made to make your home a better, more relaxed place to live. Don't forget to smile!

Another simple yet rewarding place to begin the decluttering process is pen jars. Most of us have a jar or bag of pens and pencils somewhere in the home that has likely grown significantly in size over the years. Take the time now to empty the full jar or bag and go through them. Keep a piece of scrap paper by your side to determine which writing utensils are still in good working condition. Those that are broken or no longer write will be tossed. Once you have completed testing all of your pens and pencils and now most likely have "work" and "don't work" piles, determine how many pens and pencils you feel you actually need in this jar or bag. The truth is we can only use one utensil at a time to write, so rid yourself of the excess and put the rest in a donation bin.

It is simple actions with an immediate reward, such as these examples, that keep one motivated to continue minimizing their home. It feels good to get rid of the old and/or unused items. Let go of anything that no longer serves you.

IV

TAKE ACTION: STEPS TO DECLUTTERING

DECLUTTERING PROCESS

Here is your step-by-step guide to begin the decluttering process using the example of your bedroom. This is your time to be an all-star and succeed. There is no taking it slow and steady in the decluttering process, nor are there any excuses or procrastination. It's time to get down to business!

To receive a burst of enthusiasm for life, and more importantly, for your new, decluttered life, you need to dedicate at least a full day or however long it takes to your epic clear-out and clean-up! By taking on a challenge, such as your bedroom head-on in a single day, you will be more refreshed and enthused than any espresso shot could make you.

1. Get in the ZONE

When beginning the big cull, it is extremely crucial that you remove all distractions around you. This includes your cellphone, your children, your dog, etc. You must do whatever it takes: turning your phone on airplane mode and putting it away in your car, dropping your kids off at your sibling's house, or asking your best friend to look after your furry child for a day.

2. Make Your Bed

We all know that when your bed is made, not only do you feel accomplished, but your room looks about ten times cleaner, regardless of what mess may cover the floors. A clean, tightly made bed will be your beacon of hope for the day (and also may serve as your organizing station).

3. Organized Disposal

Once your bed is clean and tidy, it is time to place either boxes or bags in your room designated for donations, recycling, trash, etc. To eliminate confusion, label these so you do not waste time peering into them trying to remember if you were giving it to charity or keeping it.

4. Begin with the NOs

Here comes the exciting part! This book has surely inspired some insight on at least one thing you can part with right now, so go ahead and find that piece and let it become the first item placed into your box of donations, recycling, trash, or whatever else you wish to call it.

Have you ever noticed that when you see a street performer with some crumpled bills in his suitcase or a barista with some spare change in their cup you are more inclined to donate? This is because there is a sense that donating is what everyone else is doing. Think back for a moment on the life goals you are hoping to achieve through minimalism:

more freedom, more money, less stress—that is how everyone else who completes this process is living. Now it's your turn—toss your first tip into the jar of joyful freedom!

5. Move Onto Categories

So, if we're working on your bedroom and you have already parted with all of the obvious "no's", it is time to move on to categories, for example, clothes. This is when your beacon of hope, aka your spotless bed, becomes your new desk. Empty everything onto your bed: your drawers, your closet. It's time to conquer Everest like a boss. Don't allow yourself to feel overwhelmed, this process is meant to be enjoyed. Assure yourself this is going to be fun and exciting, not to mention extremely liberating

HELPFUL TIPS:
NO DUPLICATES

Do you have two frying pans the same size? Three phone chargers? Four plain white T-shirts?

Assess if it is really necessary for you to have duplicates of the items you have in your wardrobe or in your home. Often, we may have duplicates we are unaware of, for example, multiple measuring cups and a multi-measuring cup. Expand your lens and see how many items of yours actually have multiple uses.

DO IT ALL AT ONCE

When choosing a category of a room to declutter, commit to the entire project all at once. This process is extremely energizing and rewarding. Once you get yourself into "the zone", commit yourself to pulling out one category of your clutter, for example, your clothing, and not leaving the area (unless of course for survival: food, water, bathroom) until your job is complete. Accomplishing an entire section, space, or category all at once will inspire you to keep going on your minimalist journey.

Think back to those high school days when you would finally finish your science project or English paper. Once that responsibility was out of your hands, you felt like a million dollars. Get that productivity mindset going, put a smile on, and get it done! The following how-to guide will work for any space or category within your life you wish to declutter, but for exemplary purposes I will refer to clothing:

PILES

When sifting through your clutter (of which you should have an entire category laid out in front of you), be sure to designate spaces, bags, or boxes beside you for different piles. These piles should consist of the following: the SAVE pile, the NO pile, the MAYBE pile, the RECYCLE pile, and, of course, the DONATE pile.

SAVE

Favorite items only. The SAVE pile is only for those items which spark joy and which you consider to be among your favorites. This pile will consist of pieces you wear on a regular basis that make you feel truly confident in yourself.

NO

The NO pile is for those items you know you do not love. Particular words to describe these items may be: uncomfortable, ill-fitting, stained, stretched, worn, tired, holey, damaged, itchy, etc.

MAYBE

The MAYBE pile is meant for pieces you are not sure whether you can part with… Don't worry, keep reading, and I will convince you otherwise.

RECYCLE

If you do not wish to sell something, or feel it is in no condition to be donated, be sure to recycle it. This could apply to old, out-of-date, or damaged electronics. Do the research in your community and figure out where and how you can safely recycle such items in your town or city.

DONATION

The DONATION pile will eventually absorb everything in the NO pile; however, sometimes it makes it easier for us to discard something when we know it is off to a better home. This could be a dress you wore once to a friend's wedding or a pair of shoes you've had great times in, but know you won't be wearing anymore. Think of the fact that your lightly used clothing will bring happiness to someone else through donation—that should be motivation enough to toss some of those MAYBE's in as well.

Make habit of these steps! You'll want to go through this exercise frequently as you gradually shift into a minimalist mindset and lifestyle. It takes practice so in the following pages you will find a chart to assist you in building a routine of cleansing.

PILES				
Save/Love	No	Maybe	Recycle	Donation

PILES				
Save/Love	No	Maybe	Recycle	Donation

PILES				
Save/Love	No	Maybe	Recycle	Donation

PILES				
Save/Love	No	Maybe	Recycle	Donation

PILES				
Save/Love	No	Maybe	Recycle	Donation

PILES				
Save/Love	No	Maybe	Recycle	Donation

V

SORTING YOUR LIFE THROUGH YOUR PILES

ONCE COMPLETED

Once completed, be sure to go through all of your piles. Do this for obvious reasons, such as accidentally tossing a LOVE item in the NO pile or vice versa, but also to ask yourself learning questions....

When you go through your LOVE pile:

When sifting through your love pile, pick each piece up individually and take the time to look at it thoroughly, asking the question:

Why do I love this piece?

Your answers should fall in the areas of comfort, confidence, practicality, or frequency of wear. Notice details such as color, quality, and fabric, and understand why you love it. This simple exercise will help you become a smarter shopper in the future.

When you go through your MAYBE pile:

When you go through your MAYBE pile, be sure to ask yourself why each particular piece didn't make it into the LOVE pile. Is it not as comfortable as the loved pieces? Not as practical as the loved pieces? Not as flattering as the loved pieces? But, let me guess...you spent a lot of money on it? *Gotcha.*

A lot of the items that end up in the MAYBE pile are those we feel too guilty to part with because we spent a substantial amount of money on them, but as it turns out, they have hardly been used. Examine each piece specifically as a lesson to yourself. Understand why this piece was not a good investment to you, and vow never to make the same mistake again. Not all classrooms have four walls.

If a lesson learned is not enough for you to part with a particular piece, decide you will do whatever it takes to get some money back for it, for example, take it to a consignment store or attempt selling it online or through apps.

If you are unable to decide on an item by simply looking at it, take the time to try it on and ask yourself the following questions:

- *Do I feel comfortable?*
- *Is the fabric soft or rough?*
- *When was the last time I wore this piece?*
- *Does this piece fit the same way as when I bought it?*
- *Has washing or wear stretched the fabric out over time?*
- *Has my body shape changed, and if so, is the piece flattering on me?*
- *Does this color or colors match my skin tone?*
- *If I tailored this item, would I wear it more often?*
- *Does this piece match my needs and my lifestyle?*

When you go through your NO pile:

When you go through your NO pile, understand why each item instantly made its way there. Did you originally purchase it because it was in style, but not necessarily your style? Did someone offer it to you, and you immediately said yes without even thinking about the space it would take up?

Become conscious. Keep only what sparks joy within your soul and provides value on a regular basis.

SENTIMENTAL ITEMS

When it comes time to face Granny's teacup collection sitting on the shelf, you should have a little more ease coming into this space after you have already begun your decluttering process. Realize sentimental items such as this are only possessions which you look at, not those which provide utility or an increase in the quality of life. Unless you are sipping on her tea set on a regular basis, it does not need to be in your surroundings. That being said, if you truly love her tea set, you owe it to her to put it to good use; every day of your life is a special occasion, so there is no need to set these away not to be used. Decide if it is functional for your home; if not, perhaps it is time to part.

The truth about sentimental items is that yes, they can bring us joy, but they bring us a spark of joy only when we think about the memories attached to them. Maybe when you were younger you enjoyed admiring the teacups at your grandmother's house while she fed you her famous shortbread and told your stories about her childhood. You enjoyed spending time with her, not with her tea cups.

There should not be any guilt in parting with these items, as you know her memory and all that she brought you in life will always remain. Minimalism is about decreasing the emotional attachment to possessions to allow more room for fulfillment in your life to be achieved without tangible items

Memories are a nice place to visit, but you should never build a home there. Know that by letting go of the tangible items of your past, you can make room for new memories.

If perhaps you find it difficult to part with gifts given, understand that they were originally given to you to make you happy, and if they no longer make you happy, they are no longer serving you. Pass a gift on to someone who will be happy to receive it, and the gift in turn will keep creating smiles. A helpful exercise for parting with sentimental items such as a trinket from the *Fontana di Trevi* or a magnet from New York City is, if you wish to remember these items, take a couple of photos and upload them onto your computer or portable hard drive. If you ever feel you miss them or wish to reminisce, the folder is yours to look through.

≥ SMILE ≥

MAKE SOME MONEY

Along with the mental, spiritual, and physical benefits of minimalism can come the financial benefits, both financial benefits from stopping the process of expansion, but also due to appraising and receiving monetary value for the items you are choosing to part with.

Parting with items you spent significant amounts of money on can be difficult, because it can result in feelings of financial loss. The truth is, there are many different avenues one can take to realize some cash back for unused or unloved pieces.

Websites such as Craigslist, Kijiji, and eBay are great for selling used furniture, clothing, jewelry, and more. There are also new cellphone applications coming out every day to assist in the selling process. Sometimes all it takes is a few minutes to take photos of belongings, writing a description and setting a price. You'll be surprised at how fast things go and how simple this process really is!

VI

MAINTENANCE

So, you've minimized your life down to a size that has you feeling the positive benefits in more ways than one. Perhaps you now have space in your living room to take up a daily yoga practice or have made enough money to plan a weekend getaway. Whatever it is, give yourself a good pat on the back and commit to the maintenance of your new lifestyle. The following pointers will help you stay out of the materialism danger zone.

TRIGGERS

What triggers you to want to shop or feel the need to purchase something? For example, is it shopping malls, antique shops, or Instagram?

Begin to become aware of what triggers give you the impulse to fall back into your not-so-smart habits and remove them from your life. This could mean consciously choosing not to spend your Saturdays at the mall and to fill that time with a hike instead. It could also mean unfollowing a fashion blogger on Instagram or unsubscribing from your favorite shop's mailing list.

Do what you need to do to help your mind feel free and not compelled to spend money and expand your possessions. Take control of what surrounds you to the utmost possible extent.

BENEFITS OF THE MIND

Imagine walking past a shopping center and not feeling the need or desire to walk in and purchase something…

Imagine walking through the grocery store aisles when you are hungry, but not feeling tempted in the slightest by quick and easy bags of chips or cookies...

As you minimize and simplify your life, you will come to discover a newfound discipline within the mind. Consciously practicing controlling inner urges to make purchases will allow everyday decisions to become quicker and easier. More simply put, it is the powerful thought: "*I don't need it.*"

We are faced with millions of decisions each and every day, some of which seem to present themselves on a daily basis:

What am I going to wear today?

What am I going to eat today?

Do I have enough money for this?

Should I make coffee at home or pick one up to go?

What should I prepare for dinner tonight?

Did I turn my straightener off before leaving the home?

Do any of those questions sound familiar?

Picture your mind being flooded with all of these questions that pop up each day, then imagine yourself opening up the top of your head and pulling out questions one by one and letting them go. There would be a lot more space in there, correct?

Limiting the amount of clutter in your life will result in a more organized state of being, which in turn will result in less daily decision-making. When it comes to more challenging decisions we may face on a weekly basis at work or on a monthly basis in the home, having less mental clutter will allow for clearer answers to come through in your mind.

Take the time now to write down 10–15 questions you frequently find yourself debating in your mind. These questions can be simple, stressful, or just plain silly—whatever you wish to do without!

Examples could be…

Should I buy this candy bar at the grocery store checkout?

Did I remember to water the plants yesterday?

Can I squeeze a workout in tomorrow morning?

1.

2.

3.

4.

5.

6.

7.

8,

9.

10.

11.

12.

13.

14.

15.

Look back at your questions and visualize yourself pulling them out of your mind one by one. Think of all the free space you would have! Not to mention letting go of emotional attachments associated with these thoughts, such as worrying that your dear plants are shriveling up as you type away at your office computer. Life will become more relaxed the more you can let go of.

A cluttered home leads to a cluttered mind, and a decluttered home results in a decluttered mind.

I first came to discover this in my final year of university, when I realized that every year I was extra ambitious and organized in the month of September. I had all of my outfits planned a week in advance, my daily planner was neatly marked and highlighted, and I was committed to my flash cards each evening like it was a friend's birthday; basically I had my *sh!t* together. At that time, my room was tidy, and each morning I felt as if I had been blessed with an extra half hour to 45 minutes of free time, just because

I had made a conscious effort to set myself up for success the night before. However, by the time October rolled around, I was creating a tornado of clothing in my room each morning and scrambling to decide what to wear; my planner would have been more legible if a three-year-old had scribbled in it with crayons, and *who in their right mind had time for flash cards?* The result of failing to set myself up for success and allowing the tornado of clothing to overtake my bedroom overflowed into my everyday life, creating sheer chaos.

After many seasons of Hurricane Zoey, I somehow was able to finally pinpoint that whenever my life felt chaotic, my room seemed to be a direct reflection of that, and vice versa.

The truth is when you are minimized, and organized life just becomes easier. Decisions are simpler, the mind is clearer, time is abundant, and your home looks amazing. Who doesn't want that? Understanding minimalism's benefits to the mind will assist you in maintaining this newfound lifestyle.

HELLO FREE TIME! IT'S BEEN A WHILE.

The more and more you simplify your life, the more time you have! This happens because you are limiting distractions, such as messes around your home to clean up, cluttered paperwork at your desk to sort through, etc. Sweet deal, right?

However, a concern many friends and subscribers have expressed is "What do I do with my newfound free time?"

The answer is simply: *anything you want*. The world is your oyster now, and time is yours to be spent; however, I recommend spending it on something fulfilling to you to avoid falling back into past bad habits like shopping. If you are at a loss for some ideas to help you discover your passions, here are some productive, self-improving ways to inspire you to stay out of tempting places like the mall and to do something beneficial for yourself:

MINDFULNESS

Have you ever meditated? We know it is good for us, but the most common excuse for not meditating is, "I don't have the time." NOW is your time. There is nothing more important than your mental health; and when you are happy, the world around you begins to fall into place perfectly. How do you feel when amazing synchronicities start to appear and every day feels like a gift? *Truly happy*. You owe it to yourself to build, maintain, and grow the connection between your mind, body, and soul. Make it happen with this newfound free time.

FITNESS

Are you physically active? I don't mean do you walk to work every day, or walk your dog; I mean something more along the lines of having a weekly routine that challenges you and makes you grow, both mentally and physically.

If you don't, now is the time to invest in your long-term health. You have one life here in this beautiful body—strive to make it the most comfortable, luxurious, and vibrant place there is.

You deserve the Ritz Carlton of homes for your intricate mind and courageous soul—make it happen.

Already into fitness? Great, it's time for a challenge. Sign up for a half marathon, a full marathon, or any type of fitness competition. Bettering your body naturally betters your mind, improves self-confidence, and inspires you to step outside of your comfort zone. Now is your time to shine.

LANGUAGE

Have you ever felt intrigued and mesmerized by a language? For me, this was and continues to be the Italian language. Hearing Italian spoken around me instantly steals my focus and transports me to *la dolce vita*. If there is a language that tickles your fancy, or which is spoken by a country you aspire to visit, learn it. The brain and mind expand significantly when you learn a new language, and it opens the door to limitless possibilities. Enrich yourself and have fun in the process by setting language goals for yourself, self-teaching, or getting yourself a tutor or a language practice partner. Learning a new language is priceless, entertaining, and rewarding. Get fulfilled and then filled with *pasta pomodoro con basilico*.

TRAVEL

Where do you dream of visiting?

Minimalism will help this dream to become more and more of a reality. Begin by planning and visualizing. Even if you cannot initially take the time off to travel or do not have the funds to embark on your dream vacation, don't hesitate, just take the first steps.

Hold your goal in your mind and plan anyway—the more you can focus and carve out the details of your dream trip, the sooner you will attract your desires into your life through your newly improved and freed mind.

VOLUNTEERING

If you had the time to help anyone, who would it be? As the minimizing process goes on, you will understand more and more how good it feels to donate to those less fortunate or who may derive more benefit from your possessions than you did.

Fill, or should I say fulfill, your free time by volunteering for an organization that draws your interest and aligns with your values. This could be spending a couple of hours a week at a local animal shelter, or offering your services on a volunteer basis to someone who could benefit from them.

Volunteer work can be extremely gratifying and inspiring, and may lead to numerous connections in life. It is true that when we give, we get back tenfold. Donating your most precious resource, time, will inspire you as well as those around you.

BUSINESS

Do you have a business venture on the brain—something you would like to start, build, and grow? Such an experience can be extremely rewarding, and there are truly no "fails", as we are always granted a lesson.

Even if you do not have a business idea in mind, the minimizing process can often be so inspiring that you will find yourself sparked with multiple ideas. Let the creativity flow into your decluttered mind. Your time is now.

ART

Do you have a creative side? When you were younger, did you lose yourself in painting, drawing, or even sculpting Play-Doh?

Rediscover your talents, or at least make more time for them. Your creativity is important, and expressing this side of yourself will reopen a part of your mind you may have left back in your childhood years. Lose yourself in the wonders of creativity, and let your emotions flow into your projects.

NATURE

There is no wi-fi in the forest, but I promise you will find a better connection. We live in an incredible world with vibrant plants and fascinating animals—how often do you take the time to experience this?—

Begin taking peaceful walks, sitting in nature, or planning hikes. Surrounding yourself with the beauty the world has to offer will not only be a literal breath of fresh air, but will allow you to feel more grounded and aware of your impact on the world as a consumer.

HOBBY

Have you always wanted to learn how to take good photos? Why not sign up for a photography class, or take the time to teach yourself the art of the image? We are living in a time when there are a lot of resources for knowledge available at our fingertips from the comfort of our very own homes!

The more you notice your inner self improving, the easier and more rewarding the journey of minimalism will become.

Try out new hobbies or habits you know will benefit you from the inside out. When you feel fulfilled and joyous about these new pursuits, It will remind you how little it can take to enjoy life, rather than feeling like you need to keep up with everyone around you.

Be your own person and become your truest self-more and more every single day.

DID I MISS ANYTHING?

Take the time now to write about all the things you would do if you had more free time in your life. The more visualization you do, the more motivation you will have to get down to business and minimize!

_____

_____

_____

_____

_____

_____

_____

_____

_____

_____

_____

DECLUTTERING FRIENDSHIPS

With this newfound lifestyle you will most likely draw attention to yourself: the good, the bad and the curious. People will notice a happier, more joyful and a more organized YOU, among many different things. As you pursue the journey of living intentionally and making more conscious decisions on a daily basis, this consciousness has no choice to expand into other areas of your existence, including who you choose to spend your precious free time with.

Lessening our literal baggage and simplifying our lives will allow our true goals and aspirations to present themselves into our lives in a clearer state. With life's vision in mind clearer each day we have no choice but to recognize who helps us along and who hinders us in this process of growing through life and not just going through life.

Begin to take note of who you feel inspired to be around, who lifts you up and who motivates you to burst out of bed in the morning and conquer goals. Surround yourself with these people and these people only.

The action of choosing to live an intentional and authentic life will most likely require the action of decluttering friendships in your life. Perhaps you already know who you leave lunches with feeling inspired by and who you leave lunches with feeling drained by so now it is time to act.

For example, let's say you have a friend named Susan. Susan has been your friend since elementary school and has remained your friend throughout your entire life because you work similar schedules and live down the street from each other. The thing about Susan is she can be extremely blunt. Blunt to the point that at times it causes you to question decisions in your life, as little as what you ate for dinner last night or as big as who you decided to marry.

Every interaction with Susan whether it be coffee, dinner or a walk around the block always leaves you feeling drained, somewhat stressed or anxious and too often, emotionally hurt.

Susan is definitely not the best person to surround yourself with. Perhaps it is convenient to have a relationship with her because of the lives you lead, but in reality, you would rather spend your precious time with people who inspire you or encourage you to pursue what matters to you most. If you took Susan out of the equation and replaced it with quality alone time or a more positive influence in the form of a friendship, take the time to consider the positive effect it would have on your life.

You deserve to live your grandest life. Know this and always remind yourself of this. Begin to use your minimalist lens to decipher who adds value to your life and who takes away from your life. Imagine the amount of personal growth and development you would be able to achieve only surrounding yourself with people who encourage your authentic life path. Continue to pursue your best version of you.

MINIMALISTS IN A MAXIMALIST WORLD

It can be difficult to dare to be different in a world that shoves things you "should" want or have in your face every day. This newfound minimalist lens often enables you to see even more clutter around you, including in the belongings of family, friends, co-workers, etc.

When I first began the journey of minimalism, I began to get so enthused about having fewer and fewer items in my wardrobe and room that I tried to introduce everyone and their mothers, fathers, and pets to this newfound lifestyle. If there's one thing I've learned about other people through minimalism, it is, *"You can lead a horse to the water, but you cannot make it drink,"* Meaning you can tell someone anything and everything you have learned through minimalism, but to reach them, it takes their being personally influenced enough for a switch to flip on in their minds. Often someone will not begin to explore minimalism until it is "their" idea. This could happen through you showing them how chic a capsule wardrobe can be or how you've saved enough money for an amazing trip, or simply seeing your immaculate home. Once someone experiences that special spark of inspiration, they will explore simplification for themselves. Stay patient. Stay chic.

A question I am often asked is, "What if your significant other or family are not minimalists and you have to live with them?"

If this is the case for you, the only option is to remain true to yourself. This journey is about you. If you respect your own journey of minimalism and truly see and feel the benefits, that is all you need. Live and let live; let the others be, and I promise it will only be a matter of time before your new lifestyle begins to rub off on them.

If you must share close living spaces with people like that and find yourself tidying up their messes, or feeling a little overwhelmed by their maximalist lifestyle, you can begin to kindly educate them about their quantity of belongings and ask them if they truly need and use all the items surrounding them.

One example of this could be your mother's kitchen. Let's say she has more than enough dishes in her cupboards as well as specialty food makers that have rarely been used. Ask her if she would like to take part in an organization day where you will help her go through her cupboards and declutter them. You will most likely help reduce the stress in her life, and in turn, you will both have a day of bonding! Offer to help your loved ones, and watch them make positive changes that will result in better choices.

Daring to be different can be challenging, but through this journey you will become a much stronger person mentally. Why spend your life striving to fit in when you know you will be most comfortable being true to yourself? Be you, perfectly you, without any excess baggage.

Dare to be different

VII

HELPFUL TIPS FOR A CLEAN HOME

How good does it feel to return home from your day to a breathable, clean and airy space? It allows you to have the relaxing evening you deserve, and to decompress after your day. In this section you will find helpful tips on keeping your newly decluttered home clean.

EVERYTHING DESERVES A HOME

Just like you and me, your possessions also deserve and should have a comfortable home. If you appreciate and love all the things you own, you will give each of them a proper home. By establishing a home for all of your belongings, you will rid yourself of the need to search for items, and this simple rule will help you keep all spaces clutter-free.

DONATION BOX

Donate, don't accumulate! Dedicate a box, tucked away in a closet or cabinet in your home, which can serve as a donation box. This box will be open for donations at all times, and you can then make monthly trips (or as many as needed) to drop off these culled items. Once you have a box dedicated to this in your home, when you come across something in your home which no longer gives you a spark of joy, it will be easy to give it away.

MAKE YOUR BED

It sounds quite simple, but did you know that making your bed every morning can profoundly change your life? How you start your day and spend your morning has lasting effects throughout the entire day. Making your bed as soon as you get up means starting your day off in a disciplined and productive way. It also sets the tone for you to keep your entire space clean as you get ready for the day. Lastly, if you don't know this already, you'll notice that when your bed is made, the entire room appears a lot cleaner!

SURFACE CHECKS

Conduct regular surface checks throughout the day. Surface checks include scanning all the surfaces within your home, such as the bedside table, dresser, desk, kitchen table, etc. Make a conscious effort to keep these spaces clutter-free. Do not let anything pile up that doesn't need to be there; as mentioned above—everything has a home. The more and more you do this, the more it will become second nature.

COOK & CLEAN

If you're the type of person who loves to cook but hates to clean, be sure to pay attention to this tip! Instead of creating a huge feast and just leaving the dishes to pile up, try to be more conscious of cleaning while you cook. If you become efficient enough with this habit, by the time you sit down to eat your meal, the clean-up left to do afterwards will be minimal, if any.

How much more enjoyable will your meal be, knowing you don't have to clean after? Bon Appetit!

PRODUCTIVITY MINDSET

While you are watching TV, listening to an audiobook, or simply puttering around the house, clean. Plug into a productivity mindset that has you choosing smarter habits each day. Be conscious of how you are spending your time and whether you can do more for your home while you are there. Once you declutter more and more, this will be less of an issue, but take the time now to implement this positive habit.

NEVER LEAVE EMPTY-HANDED

I spent my university years working as a waitress. We were taught to always do surface scans and clear any finished or unused plates away as we entered the back of the house from the restaurant floor. Take this working rule into consideration in your home. Whenever leaving a room, do a quick scan to see if anything is left behind as you exit; this could be as simple as an empty glass of water or a book you were reading. A little goes a long way, so don't let left-behinds create clutter in your home.

NO PAPERS, NO PROBLEMS

More papers, more problems. Why is it there always seems to be a pile of papers that appears out of nowhere? Mail, receipts, post-it notes, whatever it may be, the key is to not let this just happen to your newly decluttered surfaces. Here are a few actionable tips to keep paper clutter away:

DO NOT ENTER

I like to call the first tip "DO NOT ENTER" because it is specifically that. Each time you enter your home with mail or other papers from that day, make a habit of sorting them before you go in through the front door. This could simply mean saying no to receipts as you leave the grocery store on your way home or filtering through the mail from your mailbox as you walk up to your door. Become extra conscious of what you choose to bring into your home. Sooner rather than later, this "DO NOT ENTER" paper habit will overflow into other areas of your life, allowing you to only let the joyful necessities in.

FILING

For that important paperwork or those significant receipts, have a file folder or filing cabinet to help keep papers organized and condensed into a single space. If you do keep some sort of filing system, use labeled dividers, and only keep things you know you will use in the future, since organized clutter is still clutter.

Once you organize your filing system, be sure to set a reminder for yourself (thank you Siri) to sift through your papers every two to three months and recycle those which are no longer valid or needed.

OH, MAIL NO!

Oh, hell no! Unless it is checks, we do not want mail. Help the environment and yourself by switching to paperless billing for your bank statements, cellphone bills, etc. Often you can set up automatic bill payments from your online banking system. Take advantage of what technology has to offer these days, and slap that "NO JUNK MAIL" sign on your mailbox!

PICK A "REFRESH" DAY

Pick a day of the week when you are normally free to do all the household chores such as laundry, vacuuming, and dusting. Dedicate this day to being a "refresh" day, a day that sets you up for success for the week ahead. By having all the things out at once—the vacuum, window cleaner, and dirty laundry— you have the ability to put them all back once your tasks are completed to reveal the most sparkling of sanctuaries. Setting aside this day will also help lead to the rewarding habit of putting everything back in its home location when you are done using it.

VIII

GIFT GIVING & GIFT RECEIVING

So you love this new life of not acquiring anything that does not provide value or spark joy in your soul, but what happens during the holiday season? Here are some helpful tips for you to make the most out of the gift-giving seasons or days of the year.

VOICE YOUR DESIRES

Minimalism is about taking control of your life. Exercising this in different ways, such as voicing your desires, is a great practice on the way to becoming more confident in yourself. At gift-giving time, whether it be during the winter holidays or your birthday, if you know what you need or what would add exceptional benefits to your life, go ahead and ask for it. Gift-giving is about the good feelings one receives from giving—why not increase the giver's positive emotions with your positive reaction when you open something of fantastic value to you?

WHAT TO ASK FOR

Voicing your desires can be easy if you know exactly what you need in your life; for example, an upgrade on your blender because yours is barely functioning, or a vacuum for your new apartment. When asking for a specific gift, be sure to evaluate the "needs" in your life rather than the "wants." If you know your car needs an oil change around the time of your birthday, but you really want a new pair of shoes, ask yourself what is necessary for your everyday life. Needs will always trump wants.

If you can't seem to come up with anything tangible you would like to receive as a gift, experiences are always a great idea. Experiences are an opportunity for you to create lasting memories with friends or family. Experience gifts could be as small as a walk in the park with a cup of tea or as extravagant as skydiving. Moments are more important than things, so when you have the chance to choose, create memories.

If you don't feel there are any needs or experiences that you want in your life, or if you are simply looking for something fulfilling, ask your loved ones to donate to a charity of your choice as a gift. This option is fantastic and will grant the organization in need resources, as well as giving you and your loved ones the fulfillment of giving.

TO GIVE

Too often we get swept up in the buzz of Black Friday or holiday sales, when if we simply stick to either what our intended gift recipients need in their lives or what would bring them joy in their lives, we could please everyone. So what should we give, and how can we give someone something that will increase joy their lives?

CONSUMABLES

Consumables are a fantastic gift idea, because these are products or items that the gift receiver can use in their entirety. Consumables can include candles, foods, or some special wine or liquor. Does someone special in your life love a specific Tuscan wine? Treat them to a bottle you know will be savored to the last drop.

EXPERIENCES

Is there an experience you know your gift receiver would love? Is it a meal at their favorite restaurant, or a nostalgic trip to a theme park you know they would really appreciate? Moments mean more than material possessions, because memories last a lifetime. Surprise the gift recipient in your life with a well-thought-out experience you know will put a smile on their face.

NECESSITIES

Necessities are specific things you know your gift recipient needs, for example: Does the smoothie-lover in your life need a new blender? Does the music lover in your life need new headphones? Invest in a gift you are sure will create ease and enjoyment in their everyday life.

GIFT CARDS

Ultimately, if you cannot decide what to get for someone else, but want to spend money on something for them, gift cards are a great option, especially when they respect the individual's needs. Examples of this would be gift cards for the grocery store, gas station, or their favorite restaurant. Showing you care and are aware that this person could use some financial help in these areas can go a long way, and of course, can make them smile.

IX

MINIMALIST FOR LIFE: A NEW LENS

Ask yourself how life would feel for you if you felt free from comparison; free from thoughts or feelings telling you that you need to keep up with the actions of others.... This could be in the form of spending money on products you don't need, or spending time in places you would rather not be in, just to prove your success to others.

Minimalism is both a journey and a lifestyle. The longer you travel down this path, the more you will be able to make more conscious choices for your well-being. This includes, but is not limited to: clothing, grocery shopping, diet, relationships etc. Choose a life that feels best for *you*. Follow *your* bliss.

The key to maintaining this lifestyle is to live intentionally and shop consciously. People are often concerned about maintaining a minimalist lifestyle, but in reality, the benefits gained along the way will encourage you to keep moving. The positive affects you receive from conscious choices and discipline will power the positive mindset needed to pleasantly continue a life of happiness with less.

Have you ever noticed that when you buy your cat a new bed, they like the cardboard package it came in better? Or how your kids want to play with the bubble wrap their brand-new bike came packaged in? Minimalism is that simple. Sometimes joy is achieved through the simplest of items and times. Take the time now to look through your lens and choose to live each day intentionally, making conscious choices in what you choose to surround yourself with and welcome into your life.

As this book comes to an end, let's bring it back to the very beginning; perhaps we were all born minimalists, but somewhere along the path we all became distracted by shiny cars, owning the latest trends, or showing off to friends to elicit their praise or envy. Start now—start unbecoming all of the things you thought you needed to be successful, beautiful, or joyful, and know you are all of those without the help of material possessions. I like to think of my own transformation into the journey of minimalism as my new lens, or perhaps it had always been my lens, it just needed to be cleaned, polished and readjusted along the way. Clean, polish and readjust your own lens. From now on choose to live intentionally and make conscious decisions based off of what you desire your dream life to be.

You do not need a certain type of clothing or brand to feel good about yourself, strike up conversations, or impress people. You are unique and attractive in your own ways. Minimalism will uncover even more beauty about yourself that perhaps you did not see before, or that you had buried beneath excess belongings. With less clutter in your life, whether it be in the form of possessions, people, social media, the need for approval, etc., simplicity will allow you to feel content in a state of *being* rather than having.

Once you do not look to or rely on external sources or possessions to grant you happiness, you will come to realize it was within you all along. You spark your own joy and anything you choose to invite in your life should only compliment that.

The journey is yours to connect with and discover, and as you proceed, it will become clear what and who adds value to your life and what and who takes away from it. What adds value to your life will spark feelings of joy and result in continual happiness. What takes away from your life will not contain a spark, but will hold feelings of unfulfillment, stress or even anxiety.

Actively choose to live your best life.

CONCLUSION

I hope you are inspired to take part in a minimalist journey. I also hope this book has opened your mind a little wider and has sparked and inspired you to declutter your life to make more time and space for the things you love.

Through the entire process, never forget that this journey is entirely your own, and everyone's journeys will be different. If the goal of the minimalism journey that I have explained to you was to minimize your entire life until you had nothing, you would probably find yourself naked in the wilderness somewhere, and unless you are participating in the TV show Naked and Afraid, that should never be your goal. Go easy on yourself, stay motivated and inspired, and simply surround yourself with only those things that you truly love. Participate in the journey and you will be granted one amazing and joyful life. Thank you for letting me be a part of it.

Volare,
Zoey

Some last inspiration to get you started....

50 THINGS TO GET RID OF RIGHT NOW

1. The other side of a pair of lost earrings

2. Necklaces and bracelets with broken clasps

3. Rusty jewelry

4. Ticket stubs / Travel brochures / Old boarding passes

5. Dried flowers

6. Magazines

7. Hair elastics that have lost stretchiness or hair accessories you don't use

8. Little knickknacks that take up too much space

9. Kitchen utensils you don't use or have duplicates of

10. Hats you never wear

11. Clothes that don't fit

12. Old, stained, frayed towels

13. Old makeup (it's not healthy for you anyways!)

14. Expired or sample-sized toiletries

15. Expired food (check sauces & spices!)

16. Expired medication

17. Toys your pets don't play with

18. Excess toys your children won't miss

19. Scratched nonstick cookware

20. Old underwear

21. Stockings with runs

22. Worn-out sheets, bedding and pillows

23. Near-empty bottles of cleaning products
    (clean then recycle!)

24. Extra buttons that come with newly purchased clothes

25. Wedding invites / Save-the-dates /Wedding favors
    you don't use

26. Broken kitchen equipment or kitchen equipment
    you don't use

27. Furniture manuals or manuals in general (everything can
    be available online and how-to videos are awesome!)

28. Unused vases

29. Random containers and jars

30. Lunch containers with missing lids

31. Unused or damaged stationery, stickers, and
    sticky notes

32. Old artwork or old children's artwork

33. Extra and unused coffee mugs

34. Damaged or chipped glasses

35. Cards or gifts from exes (ditch the bad juju!)

36. Frequent shopper cards you never use (while you're at it unsubscribe from all those shopping emails!)

37. Magnets

38. Broken Christmas decorations or Christmas lights that don't work

39. Old and outdated software on your computer

40. Old cell phones and their unused accessories

41. Hand-me-downs that you're guilt-tripped into keeping

42. Freebie or promotional t-shirts you never wear

43. Pajamas you never gravitate towards

44. Old planners or calendars

45. Completed journals or notebooks left unused

46. Old school books you'll never use again

47. Pens or pencils sitting in a jar among many

48. Old or unused tools, nails and screws

49. Damaged or odds and ends of gift wrapping

50. Limiting beliefs

AUTHOR

Zoey Arielle Poulsen, better known by her wildly popular
YouTube channel: Zoey Arielle, is a twenty-five-year-old
Canadian girl living life the way it was meant to be lived. She
is currently working remotely in Rome, Italy. Zoey was born
and raised on Vancouver Island, BC, Canada and relocated
to Toronto to pursue a post-graduate degree and career in
Sport & Event Marketing, where she spent a few enjoyable,
transformational years. Zoey felt alive in the big city of Toronto,
yet noticed time seemed to escape her as she spent the majority
of her time sitting at a desk. Her zest for life and willingness to
take chances drove her to follow her dreams of living in Rome,
Italy. Zoey now lives a life well-travelled and shares her positive

message with the world through her YouTube channel and books. By sharing her voice and vulnerabilities with the world, she's become the digital nomad of sorts we've all come to love.

CPSIA information can be obtained
at www.ICGtesting.com
Printed in the USA
BVOW09s0451211217
503291BV00003B/4/P